POLITICAL Bollocks

How to talk your way into government...

First published in 2010. A catalogue record for this book is available from the British Library

ISBN: 978-1-844259-98-4

Published by Haynes Publishing, Sparkford, Yeovil, Somerset BA22 7JJ, UK
Tel: 01963 442030 Fax: 01963 440001 Int. tel: +44 1963 442030 Int. fax: +44 1963 440001
E-mail: sales@haynes.co.uk Website: www.haynes.co.uk

Haynes North America Inc., 861 Lawrence Drive, Newbury Park, California 91320, USA

All images © Mirrorpix

Creative Director: Kevin Gardner

Packaged for Haynes by BrainWave

Printed and bound by J F Print Ltd., Sparkford. Somerset

POLITICAL Bollocks

How to talk your way into government...

Richard Havers

There was a time when we looked upon our politicians as god-like geniuses; men and women who had a command of the English language that put us mere mortals to shame.

'Political Speak' is an art – the art of never saying anything that may come back to haunt you – at least not intentionally. Politicians must be given some very special training at which they learn the black arts of talking complete boll**ks, while managing to sound utterly plausible. Ask yourself a simple question. Has any politician ever answered a straight question with a straight answer?

Recently the scandal over MPs expenses has raised the political boll**cks bar to dizzying new heights. MPs of all shades, all ages and even both sexes in attempting to clear both the bar and their name have attempted intellectual summersaults of mind-boggling difficulty while justifying their actions. Some, of course, have just talked complete boll**ks.

Then again as someone once said, "politics is show business for ugly people." But perhaps what all that proves is that there's been far too much show business and not enough business being done on our behalf – although many MPs with second and even third jobs may not agree. Perhaps it's this ever closer relationship between politicians and business that has given rise to an increasing number of our politicians sounding like middle-managers (clearly more and more of them look like middle managers).

At MP training camp they are told never to comment on the hypothetical, but all too often some wily media type tricks them into doing just that. The consequences are usually catastrophic for the politician and often hilarious for the rest of us.

If you want to talk your way into government some of what's inside may help, the rest will remind you how easy it is to come a cropper on the slippery political slope. We are about to have the largest influx of men and women into Westminster who have never before served as elected Members of Parliament. They, and many other politicians, would do well to heed George Orwell's words written in 1946 under the title, 'Politics and the English Language'.

* Never use a metaphor, simile, or other figure of speech which you are used to seeing in print.

* Never use a long word where a short one will do.

* If it is possible to cut a word out, always cut it out.

* Never use the passive where you can use the active.

* Never use a foreign phrase, a scientific word, or a jargon word if you can think of an everyday English equivalent.

* Break any of these rules sooner than say anything outright barbarous.

If many of our politicians followed his advice they would of course be struck dumb...

For too long, decisions have been taken behind closed doors — tablets of stone have simply been passed down to people without bothering to involve people, listen to their views or give them information about what we are doing and why.

Peter Mandelson

A government of all the talents.

It needs to
be said that
the poor
are poorer,
because
they don't
have enough
money.

Keith Joseph

It isn't pollution
that's harming the
environment. It's the
impurities in our air and
water that are doing it.

Dan Quayle

The aim of the SPN is to provide an online forum for focused discussion of a diverse range of social, economic and governance issues, and to support and supplement face-to-face dialogue rather than to take its place. Thus people who have met can use it to continue their discussions, and groups that form online may subsequently meet in person.

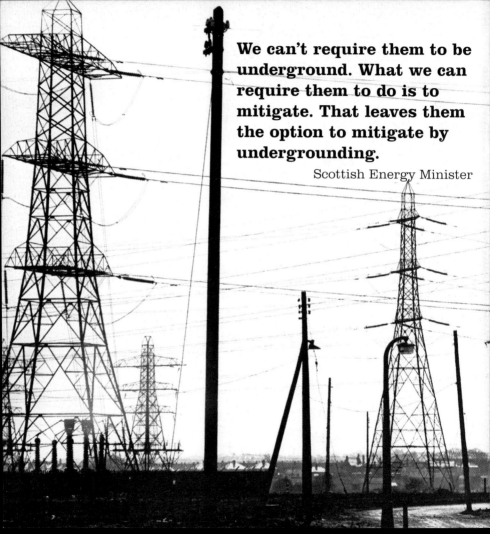

We can't require them to be underground. What we can require them to do is to mitigate. That leaves them the option to mitigate by undergrounding.

Scottish Energy Minister

A consensus politician is someone who does something that he doesn't believe is right because it keeps people quiet when he does it.

John Major

**Politics
is the art
of saying
things
that sound
plausible
and sensible
while at the
same time
being totally
at odds with
reality.**

The claims I made were in accordance with the rules, and were all approved by the fees office.

Peter Viggers on his duck house

I am doing nothing wrong whatsoever. I am using it for parliamentary purposes. It is legitimate and proper in accordance with the rules laid down by the fees office.

Just about any MP caught out in the expenses scandal

Our hard working young people are a credit to Great Britain.

Just about any politician trying to ingratiate themselves with young voters

Diversity – especially cognitive diversity – is critical to the continuing success of the creative industries.

Report on Britain's creative industries

We are not legislating now on the basis that we are bringing it in now for something that might happen in the future; we are bringing in a position for if it becomes unhypothetical. But it won't be hypothetical if and when it happens.

Jacqui Smith

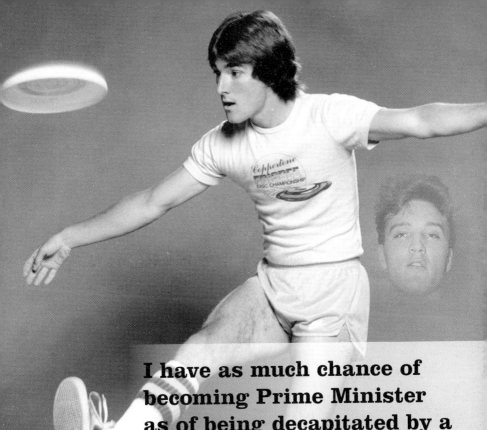

I have as much chance of becoming Prime Minister as of being decapitated by a frisbee or of finding Elvis.

Boris Johnson

I think that most people who have dealt with me think that I am a pretty straight sort of guy — and I am.

Tony Blair

At least 50 per cent of the population are women, and the rest are men.

Harriet Harman

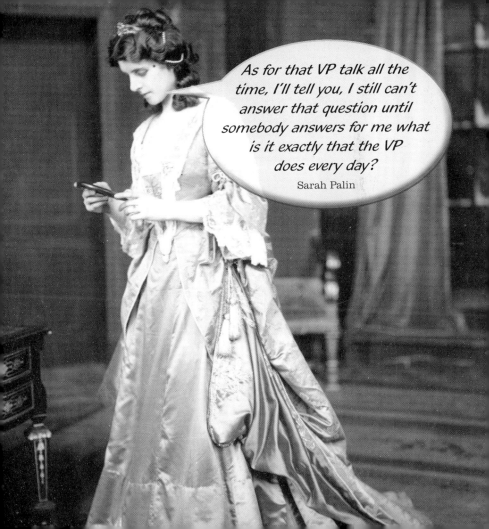

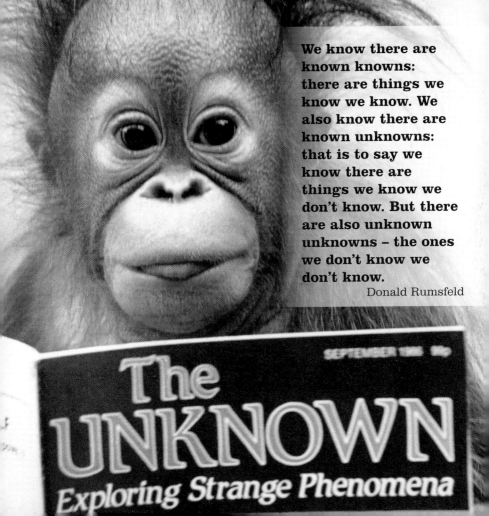

We know there are known knowns: there are things we know we know. We also know there are known unknowns: that is to say we know there are things we know we don't know. But there are also unknown unknowns – the ones we don't know we don't know.

Donald Rumsfeld

SEPTEMBER 1996 80p

The UNKNOWN
Exploring Strange Phenomena

I think that gay marriage should be
between a man and a woman.

The Governor of California, Arnold Schwarzenegger

The best argument against democracy is a five-minute conversation with the average voter.

Winston Churchill

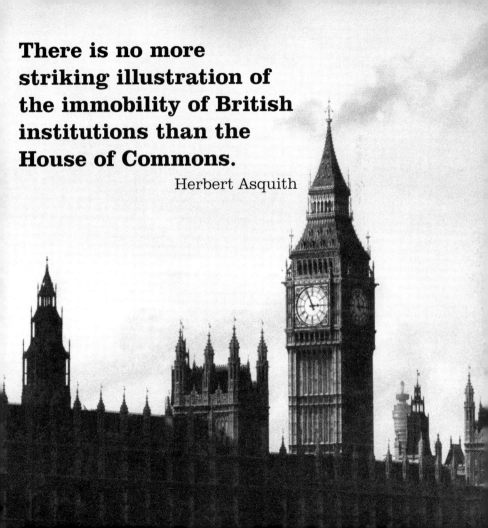

There is no more striking illustration of the immobility of British institutions than the House of Commons.

Herbert Asquith

Anybody who enjoys being in the House of Commons probably needs psychiatric help.

Ken Livingstone

John Prescott
is proof the 11+
system worked,
he failed!

Anon

The older I get the more passionate I become about ageism.

Robin Cook

Who is to blame for the riots? The rioters are to blame. Who is to blame for the killings? The killers are to blame.

Al 'Mr Climate Change' Gore.

I don't think
I would use
the word
greedy, but
I think we
went over
the top a bit.
Neil Hamilton MP

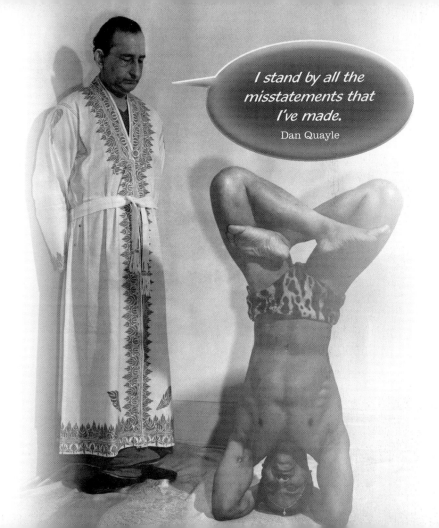

I believe in transparency.

Any Minister caught trying to hide something

Take the x out of expert and what do you have? A drip under pressure!

There are no half measures in our blueprint for the future.

Jack McConnell

We do know of certain knowledge that Osama bin Laden is either in Afghanistan, or in some other country, or dead.

Donald Rumsfeld

I want to see the government consultation process reformed... we should give the people of Scotland the facts, meet them face to face, ask their opinion and then tell them the truth.

Liberal Democrats 2007 Scottish election manifesto

The future, where most of us are destined to spend the rest of our lives.

Geoffrey Howe

Regarding his travel expenses, the MP said he needed to drive around his constituency throughout the year. He said that he recorded his mileage precisely and was sometimes forced to make three return journeys between Westminster and Hendon in a single day!

"This is your pot, sat on a shelf in the Fees Office, and our job is to make sure you have it as it's part of your salary because no one here since the time of Cromwell has had the guts to address MPs' remuneration", you can't blame the older MPs for not giving due diligence to what it was spent on. The system was an utter disgrace, but it was the system.

Nadine Dorries MP

And what I want to argue is that the joining of these two forces — the information revolution and the human urge to co-operate for justice — makes possible for the first time in history something we have only dreamt about: the creation of a truly global society.

Gordon Brown

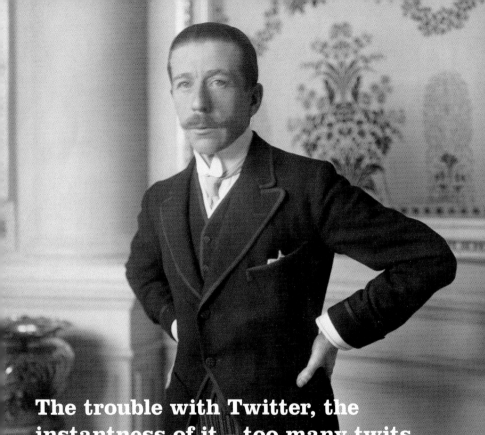

The trouble with Twitter, the instantness of it – too many twits might make a twat.

David Cameron

I don't mind how much my Ministers talk, so long as they do what I say.

Margaret Thatcher

There are more crimes in Britain now, due to a huge rise in the crime rate.

Neil Kinnock

Mussolini never killed anyone. Mussolini used to send people on vacation in internal exile.

Silvio Berlusconi

Political correctness is a doctrine, fostered by a delusional, illogical minority, and rabidly promoted by an unscrupulous mainstream media, which holds forth the proposition that it is

entirely possible to pick up a turd by the clean end.

The 2007 winning entry from an annual contest at Texas A&M University for a definition of a political term

We have a lot of kids who don't know what work
means. They think work is a four-letter word.

Hilary Clinton

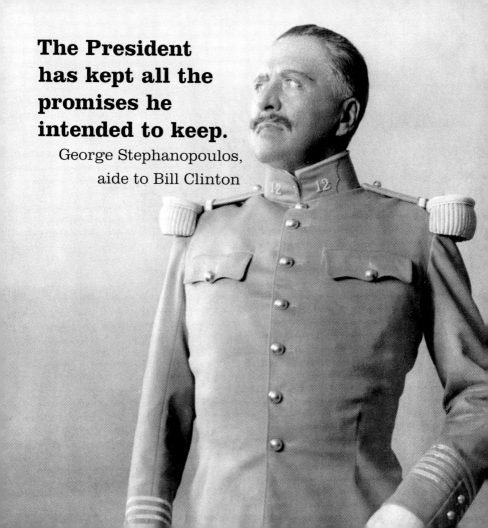

The President has kept all the promises he intended to keep.

George Stephanopoulos, aide to Bill Clinton

Our challenge is two-fold: First to ensure the rapid implementation across Government and the public services of the many efficiency savings that have already been identified, but not effectively delivered. And secondly to embed the process of constant innovation in our public sector to

create a culture in which the pursuit of efficiency becomes self-sustaining. To help me in these tasks, we have decided to establish a Shadow Public Services Productivity Advisory Board.

A Conservative Shadow Chief Secretary of the Treasury

It's only fair to point out that the relationship between the political leader and his or her spin doctor is always special.

Jackie Ashley, journalist

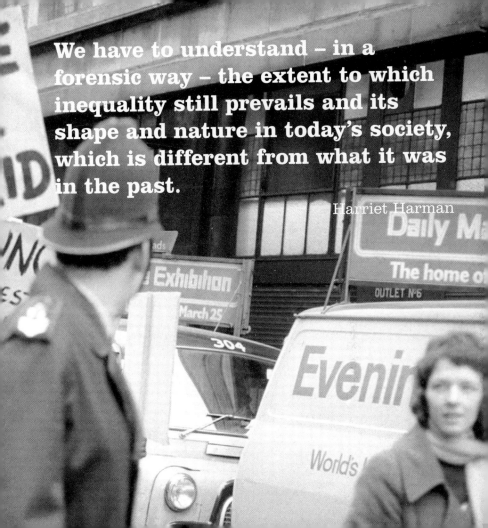

We have to understand – in a forensic way – the extent to which inequality still prevails and its shape and nature in today's society, which is different from what it was in the past.

Harriet Harman

All the "best people" from the gentlemen's clubs, and all
the frantic fascist captains, united in common hatred
of Socialism and bestial horror at the rising tide of the
mass revolutionary movement, have turned to acts of
provocation, to foul incendiarism, to medieval legends
of poisoned wells, to legalize their own destruction of
proletarian organizations, and rouse the agitated petty-
bourgeoise to chauvinistic fervor on behalf of the fight
against the revolutionary way out of the crisis.

Communist pamphlet from the 1940s

To listen to some people in politics, you'd think 'nice' was a four-letter word.

David Steel

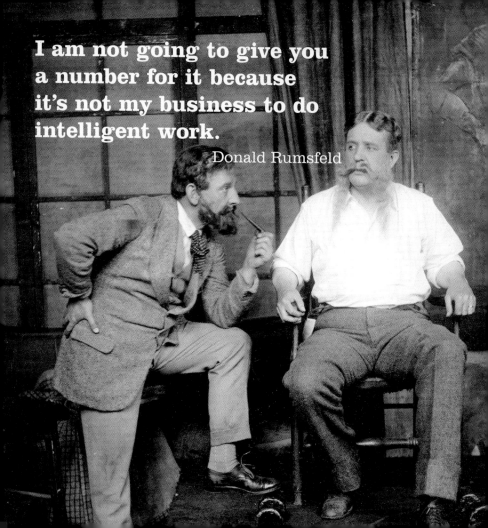

I am not going to give you a number for it because it's not my business to do intelligent work.

Donald Rumsfeld

We used to have a pint at every stop... about 10 stops in a day... we used to do that then go home for tea and then go out in the evening to the pub.

William Hague

Flipper!
Any one of huge numbers of MPs profiteering from the
loopholes in the Parliamentary expenses system

That was not a genuine Question Time; that was a lynch mob.

Nick Griffin

We have witnessed the Prime Minister's remarkable transformation in the last few weeks from Stalin to Mr Bean.

Vince Cable

We must give every child
a fair start in life.

Nick Clegg

Mrs Thatcher's silence has resounded like thunder across Britain.

Paddy Ashdown

There's no smoke without mud being slung around.

Edwina Currie

Margaret Thatcher adds the diplomacy of Alf Garnett to the economics of Arthur Daley.

Denis Healey

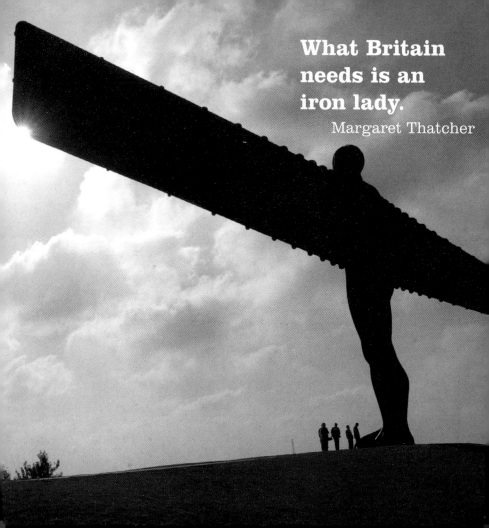

What Britain needs is an iron lady.

Margaret Thatcher